HELLO, NEW ZEALAND!

MEGAN McKEAN

Thames & Hudson

Hello, New Zealand! And *kia ora* to you!

Kia ora means 'hello' in te reo Māori,
the language of the indigenous
people of New Zealand.

Aotearoa is the Māori name for
New Zealand and means 'land of
the long white cloud'.

New Zealand is made up of two big
islands and hundreds of smaller islands.
Our country is full of wonderful and
unique creatures – just like us!
We are brown kiwi birds.

Even though we can't fly, we are
a well-known New Zealand icon.
We are so famous that people from
New Zealand are called 'Kiwis'.

Come with us on a journey from the
North to the South Island. Can you find
six of us in every place we visit?

Northland is at the top of the North Island. The Treaty of Waitangi was signed here by Māori chiefs and the British Crown in 1840.

Northland is the home of the giant kauri tree, Tāne Mahuta, which means 'god of the forest'. It is more than 2000 years old.

Ninety Mile Beach stretches out along the coast. But don't be fooled by the name – it is actually only 55 miles long.

The steep sand dunes here look more like desert than beach. Try boogie boarding all the way down them!

Auckland is New Zealand's biggest and busiest city. The Harbour Bridge stretches across the sparkling water of Waitematā Harbour.

The harbour is full of yachts, sailboats, tugs, ferries and ships. Auckland is often referred to as the City of Sails.

The black gravelly sand on Auckland's rugged west coast beaches is a mixture of rough volcanic rock and ironsand.

On hot summer days, don't forget your jandals for the dash to the water – this black sand heats up very quickly!

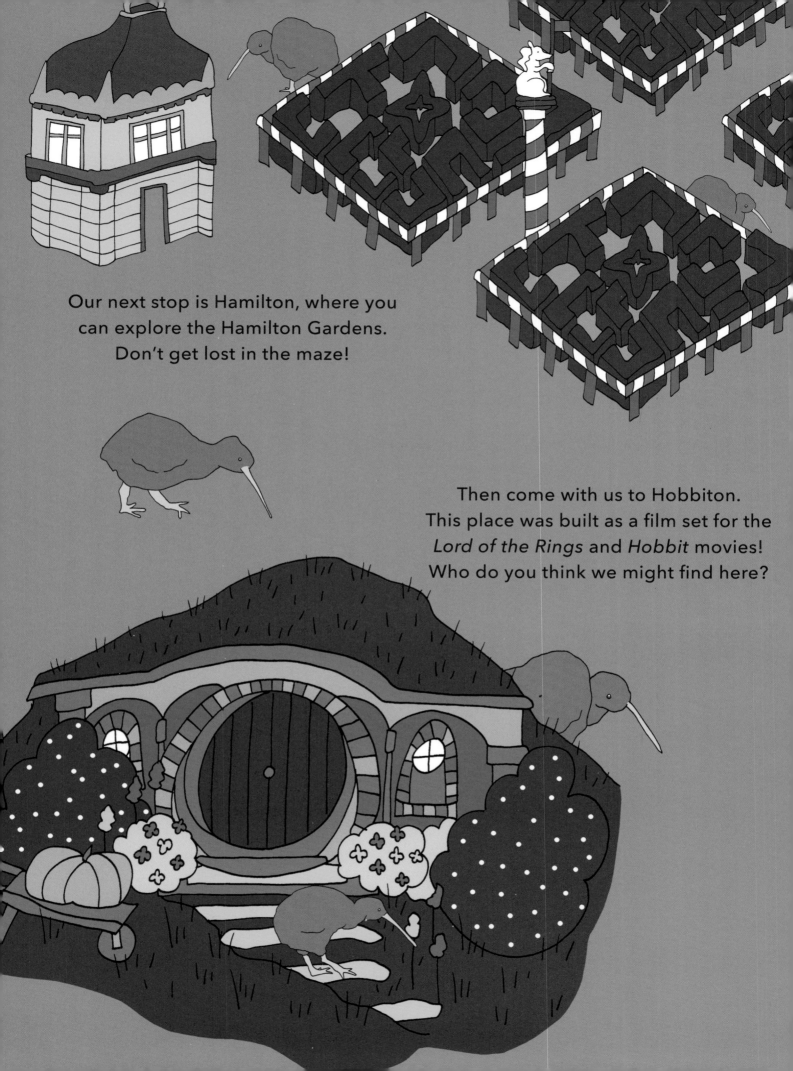

Our next stop is Hamilton, where you can explore the Hamilton Gardens. Don't get lost in the maze!

Then come with us to Hobbiton. This place was built as a film set for the *Lord of the Rings* and *Hobbit* movies! Who do you think we might find here?

In Waitomo, you can go deep underground to see limestone caves and the dazzling display of glow-worms twinkling in the dark.

At Otorohanga Kiwi House, you will find many of our extended *whānau*, or family. See kiwis in a night-time setting, and try feeding some red-crested parakeets, or *kākāriki. Kākāriki* also means 'green'.

Let's head to exciting Rotorua. Here you can walk among gigantic redwood trees and see explosive geysers shoot steaming water way up into the sky.

Sit and listen to the bubbling, hissing mud pools, and admire the steamy, cloudy hot springs and colourful volcanic rock formations.

We can see why Rotorua is called a geothermal wonderland – but it is also what gives the place its own memorable rotten-egg smell!

There are many special Māori cultural experiences to take in. Watch a haka, the fierce war dance, and try tasty, smoky food cooked in a *hangi*.

South of Rotorua is glittering Lake Taupō, New Zealand's largest lake, which is in the crater of a huge extinct volcano. Try water-skiing, kayaking, or go trout fishing to catch your dinner.

Nearby is Tongariro National Park. Hike across volcanic landscapes with craters and see the brilliant, jewel-coloured Emerald Lakes.

You might spot some of our friends, like the friendly *toutouwai*, or the energetic *piwakawaka* or fantail.

Much rarer is the *whio*, the endangered blue duck that lives in rivers and streams around Tongariro. At night-time, you might even see brown kiwis like us.

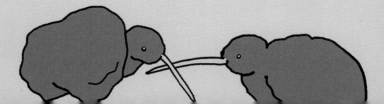

Napier is a small city on the east coast of Hawke's Bay. In 1931, an enormous earthquake destroyed most of the town.

Napier was rebuilt in the Art Deco style of the time. Look for zigzags and geometric shapes on the pastel buildings!

The National Aquarium of New Zealand is home to lots of native species, and fish from all around the world.

Meet the *tuatara*, the most ancient living reptile in the world. You can also get up close with penguins, piranhas, turtles and alligators.

Right at the bottom of the North Island is New Zealand's capital – Wellington. This city is famous for being very windy. It's sure to ruffle our feathers!

There's much to learn at the national museum, Te Papa Tongarewa. This is the only place in the world where you can see a colossal squid.

Why not hike up Mount Victoria and see all the way to the South Island? Or take a ride on the bright red 100-year-old cable car to Zealandia!

Zealandia is an eco-sanctuary for native birds, bugs and lizards. Here you can see these creatures living in their natural environment.

If you're like us and you can't
fly from the North Island to the
South Island, take the ferry instead.

A three-hour ferry trip takes
you through Wellington Harbour,
across wild Cook Strait and up
Queen Charlotte Sound to Picton.

From the observation deck are
dramatic views of the coastline.
You might even glimpse dolphins and
whales swimming alongside the ferry.

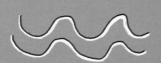

Giant albatross often fly overhead,
showing off their huge wings.
We are very envious!

Christchurch is one of the oldest cities in New Zealand and is well known for its English heritage. Many of its heritage buildings were damaged or destroyed in an earthquake in 2011.

Come punting with us on a flat-bottomed boat along the Avon River, or ride through the city streets on a heritage tram.

The TranzAlpine train passes through the snow-capped Southern Alps, through native beech forests and along the Waimakariri River.

Early Antarctic explorers began their journeys from Christchurch and they still do today. At the International Antarctic Centre you can face a freezing storm and pat a husky.

If boats and trains aren't exciting enough, come with us to Queenstown! Here you can go bungy jumping, white water rafting, or ride in a jet boat.

Nestled in the Southern Alps, Queenstown is also famous for skiing, snowboarding, skydiving and canyon swinging.

And we think the nearby mountain ranges, The Remarkables, certainly live up to their name.

Arrowtown is an historic settlement with cottages and a rich gold-mining history. You can still try your luck panning for gold in the Arrow River.

Milford Sound is a world-famous fiord. A fiord is a long, narrow inlet with steep sides carved into the mountain by a glacier.

Milford Sound is surrounded by dense rainforest. Waterfalls thunder down its high, rocky cliffs into the dark water.

It is home to fur seals, penguins and dolphins, and very rare black coral.

You might see a *kea*, New Zealand's cheeky alpine parrot. Their Māori name sounds like the call they make – a loud '*keee-aa!*'

They are very curious birds that will even play practical jokes on humans. Can you spot any *kea* flying about?

Dunedin is full of Scottish history, sometimes called the 'Edinburgh of New Zealand'. Larnach Castle is here, the only castle in the country.

On the Otago Peninsula you'll find The Royal Albatross Centre, the place to see the northern royal albatross, or *toroa*, in their natural habitat.

Toroa are the biggest seabirds in the world. Their newly hatched chicks are almost the same size as fully grown kiwis!

Down on the beach, you might see the endangered yellow-eyed penguin, or *hoiho*, and plenty of seals and sea lions.

Invercargill is one of the world's southernmost cities. It is called the 'City of Water and Light' because of its rivers – and plenty of rain...

...and because you can sometimes see the coloured lights of the breathtaking aurora australis dancing in the night sky.

The nearby fishing town of Bluff is known around the world for its *kai mōana*, or seafood. We love the famous Bluff oysters!

A short ferry trip from Bluff will take you to Stewart Island, or *Rakiura*, where you can see lots of native birds.

We couldn't finish our journey without showing you some more of our friends that you might see on your travels!

The *kakapo* is a large, moss-green, flightless parrot that lives in the forest. It only comes out at night-time and is very rare.

The *tui* is a honeyeater with a call that sounds like a robot.

The *weta* is an unusual insect that has been around since prehistoric times. It has a long body, spiny legs and curved tusks.

The *morepork* is New Zealand's only native owl.

Did you spot any of them during your trip?

We hope you enjoyed exploring New Zealand with us. *Haere rā*, goodbye, to you!

For Joshua

First published in Australia in 2019
by Thames & Hudson Australia Pty Ltd
11 Central Boulevard Portside Business Park
Port Melbourne Victoria 3207
ABN: 72 004 751 964

www.thamesandhudson.com.au

© Megan McKean 2019 (text and illustrations)

22 21 20 19   5 4 3 2 1

The moral right of the author has been asserted.

Thames & Hudson Australia wishes to acknowledge that Aboriginal and Torres Strait Islander people are the traditional custodians of this land where we live, learn, work and play.

ISBN: 978 1 7607603 6 6

 A catalogue record for this book is available from the National Library of Australia

Design: Megan McKean
Editing: Lorna Hendry
Printed and bound in China by 1010.